Sources of design

Many embroiderers get their ideas directly from the observation of flowers and plants. Others are inspired by photos, illustrations, greetings cards, advertisements, museum artifacts, china and porcelain, textiles, and even nature programmes on TV.

There are many ways of translating the idea in your mind, such as the flower on the seed packet or the plant in your garden, into an image you can use as a working drawing for embroidery. It can be done by drawing, by photography, by making tracings or photocopies or templates, or by a combination of these methods.

Drawing

Work from an actual specimen if you can, and make a sketch of the whole plant showing the habit of growth. More detailed studies can pick out special markings, tone and texture.

Even if you are not good at drawing it is still worth while attempting a few sketches, as the very act of doing so is an exercise in close observation. Simplify the outlines, with discs for flowerheads and ribs for leaves. If you pretend the plant is transparent the structure becomes clearer. After sketching and study, you will find that one aspect of the plant will appeal to

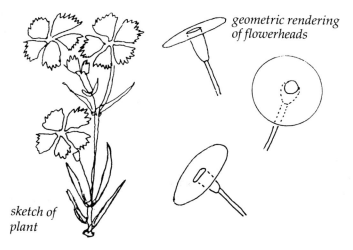

geometric rendering of flowerheads

sketch of plant

you most, and this can be adapted for your working drawing.

Photography

Take a lot of photographs from different angles, both general views and close-ups. The photos can be cut up and rearranged.

You can make tracings of the selected areas and arrange them on a background. Be selective about detail, and simplify the outlines if necessary.

love-in-a-mist flowerhead traced from a photograph

Templates from plants

Pick off a leaf or petal and trace round it, lay the tracing over several thicknesses of paper and cut it out. The resulting set of identical shapes can be arranged either side up on a coloured background. Different shapes from the same plant could be combined.

petal used as a template

Photocopying

Flowerheads and leaves can be laid directly on the glass and photocopied; a folded cloth laid over them will hold them in position and give the image a white

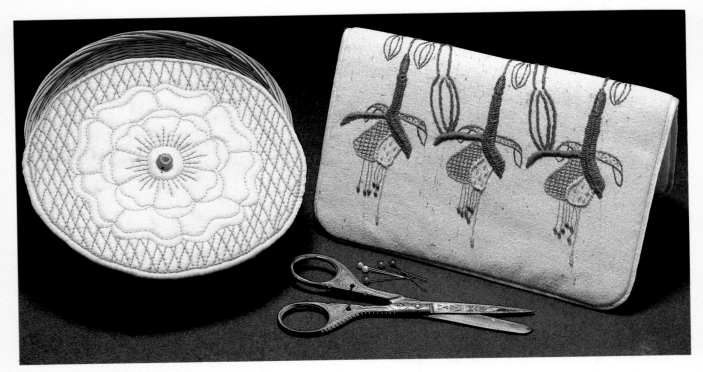

Basket cover by Kit Pyman.
Quilted Tudor rose design, transferred by needle marking round templates. Worked on silk
mixture fabric in buttonhole thread in back stitch. Backed with pelmet vilene and lined.
7 in (17 cm) diameter.

Evening bag by Molly Taylor.
Designed from drawings of fuchsias, and transferred by the sewing method. Worked on matt
heavy silk with mixed threads in surface stitches with the addition of a few beads. The bag
was stiffened with pelmet vilene and piped with shiny silk.
8 × 5½ in (21 × 14 cm).

RIGHT
Painted flowers by Carol Williams.
Design derived from pattern exercises, and transferred by direct tracing. Worked on
unbleached calico in stranded cottons. The petals were painted in with watercolours, and
then raised by stuffed quilting.
8 × 7 in (20 × 17 cm).

4

background. Although some shapes may be flattened, the general outline and markings are usually clearly reproduced and can be used as the basis of a design.

A photocopier is a great help in trying out design ideas. Images can be multiplied, cut out, rearranged, and formed into different patterns. Designs can also be enlarged or reduced.

On some photocopiers it is possible to copy on to tracing paper, which means that the image can be reversed. Some will copy on to non-woven fabrics, which can be incorporated into the embroidery.

photocopied carnation bloom

photocopied flowers and leaves from Japanese anemone

Composition

Composition is the art of arranging the elements of the design into a pleasing whole, or adapting it to fit a particular shape. Even large 'free' panels are often under some constriction of size, shape or colour. Plants can be presented as they grow, or formalised into simpler shapes. Two plants of different habits of growth will gain emphasis if used together.

Paper plan

Practical items should be carefully planned beforehand. If you make a paper mockup in the intended size, then you can try out your design in position, and check whether it looks all right and is in proportion to the scale of the article.

Geometric structure

Single motifs: draw the outline of the space you wish to fill, then with a pencil and ruler draw the central vertical and horizontal lines. Extend these into a grid. Indicate curving lines with a pair of compasses. This mass of pencilled guidelines can form the basis of your design.

Borders: in the same way, draw an outline of the space the border is to fill, and construct a grid. Flowerheads can be indicated with circles drawn round coins.

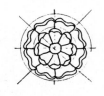

Tudor rose design for quilting

rose border

Treatment

Different techniques demand designs with different qualities. Simple shapes, as in the single Tudor rose, will adapt easily to quilting, as the petals can be divided into template shapes.

The border of the roses is formal but lends itself to interesting interpretations in surface stitchery.

The delicate spray of convolvulus consists of small narrow shapes eminently suitable for shadow work.

Once you are satisfied with your design, you can enlarge or reduce it as required.

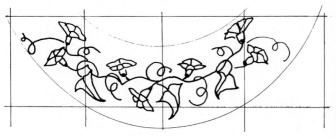

spray of convolvulus fitted into a crescent

Enlarging and reducing designs

Designs can be scaled up or down by various methods:

1. A photographic negative, or a selected area of it, can be sent for processing and the print enlarged/reduced as required.
2. A photograph, sketch, or tracing can be enlarged or reduced on a photocopier.
3. A transparency can be projected on to a sheet of paper on the wall and drawn out.

You can also alter designs yourself by the following method:-

a. Enclose your design in a square or rectangle, and trace it off.
b. Divide the area into a number of equal squares. The more detailed the design the greater number of divisions.
c. Cut a piece of paper the exact finished size of the work, and divide it into exactly the same number of squares.
d. Copy the design freehand, square by square.

On a very large item, such as a bedspread or a hanging, the redrawn grid can consist of square sheets of paper, which can be taped together and hung or laid in situ to give a clear picture of the greatly enlarged design.

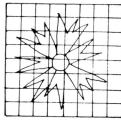 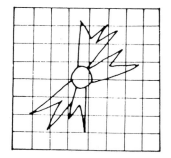

enlarging a design

Colouring fabrics and threads

Fabric paints, dyes, inks and crayons are now widely available. The opportunity to combine painting and stitchery has proved irresistable to embroiderers, and the following is a brief survey of some of the methods in current use.

Preparation: read the instructions for your chosen medium carefully before buying, as some of them only work on certain fabrics, and some are only suitable for transfers.

Equipment: you will need a few paintbrushes, a stencil brush, a board for mounting, adhesive tape, drawing pins (thumbtacks), an old pan and rubber gloves for dyeing.

Fabric: cut out a generous amount of fabric. Wash it if necessary, then iron it. Zig-zag or oversew the edges if they are likely to fray.

Stretching: many colouring techniques should be done on a smooth taut surface, so the fabric should either be framed or mounted on a board.

Thin fabrics and fine silks should be framed, (see page 30), rather than mounted, as the frame keeps the fabric from clinging to a wet background and staining.

Mount fabric on a board as follows:- lay a few sheets of newspaper on the board, cover with a sheet of white paper and tape in position. Lay the fabric down and smooth it outwards from the centre of each side, putting in drawing pins, (thumbtacks), at close intervals.

Dyeing

Choose the right dye for the fibre. Prepare the fabric as required and follow the instructions on the tin. If you wish to dye your threads as well, throw them in with the fabric. A collection of threads of different fibres will take up the colour in a rich array of related colours which will blend well. To achieve both light and dark

Foxglove by Jean Robinson.
Designed from drawings of
foxgloves, transferred by direct
tracing against window light.
Worked on transfer-printed
white sheeting in one strand of
stranded cotton in a variety of
surface stitches – stem,
buttonhole, long and short,
couching, fly, bullion knots,
back stitch, with some net
applique and stuffed quilting. A
project to explore the many
shades of colour in a foxglove,
observed in live specimens.
5 × 7 in (12 × 18 cm).

'Mexicana' by Mary Boughey.

Designed from a crayon sketch of a pot of geraniums, transferred by the template method. The polycotton background was transfer-printed, then mounted in the hoop frame and worked in rayon threads in surface stitches – fly stitch, cretan stitch and straight stitches. Both sketch and embroidery were worked very quickly to keep the piece lively rather than accurate.

10 in (25 cm) diameter.

tones, as well as colour, you will need to dye light, medium and dark threads.

Painting

Work on flat stretched fabric.

Washes of colour can be applied to wet fabric with a large brush. When this is dry, details can be put in with a fine brush. Drying can be speeded up by using a hairdryer.

Selected areas can be painted or textured, and crayons and inks can be used as well as paints.

Prints

All kinds of textures can be directly printed on to fabric. Flowers and seedheads, leaves, petals and cut buds can all be dipped in paint and pressed on the fabric. The basis of the illustration on page 12 is a mass of prints made with a poppy seed head.

Transfer prints

Choose paints or crayons suitable for transfer printing, colour your design on paper, and then iron it off on to the fabric like a transfer.

Textures can be directly transferred. Rub crayon over a leaf, (the underside is usually the most textured), lay it on the fabric, cover with a cloth, and transfer the rubbing with a hot iron.

Stencils

This is a more formal way of using paint, and useful for repeating patterns and borders. The shapes should be kept very simple.

Trace your design on to a piece of thin card or waxed stencil paper, (using the tracing method opposite). Lay it on a board and cut the design out with a sharp scalpel, working from the corners outwards. Keep the cut-out shapes, as they can be made into negative or voided designs.

Lay the stencil in position. Take a stubby stencil brush, or a cut-off old nylon brush, dip it in fabric paint and, taking off the surplus on a piece of absorbent paper, dab the dryish brush into the stencil shapes.

poppyseed print

alchemilla leaves transfer printed on to fabric

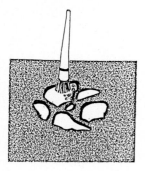

using a stencil

Poker work

This is hardly painting, but it is another method of tinting fabric. Poker pens can now be bought in craft shops, and the heat produces a variety of effects from a delicate sepia line to a deep scorch. This method is used in the illustration on page 16.

Transferring designs

Use the method of transfer recommended for your chosen technique.

First prepare the fabric. Allow a generous margin round the intended size and cut it out by the thread. Oversew or zig-zag or tape over the raw edges. Iron it if necessary. Mark central vertical and horizontal lines with running stitches.

Depending on the method of embroidery to be used, designs may be traced on to the right or the wrong side of the fabric. The original tracing can be used face down or face up.

Tracing method

Trace off your design, marking central vertical and horizontal lines. Tape the prepared fabric on to a board. Lay a piece of dressmakers' carbon face down over the fabric. Lay the tracing over the carbon, (face upwards usually), and position it carefully. Make sure all three layers are secured to the board.

Using a sharp hard pencil, trace round the design with firm pressure so that the carbon transfers the lines cleanly. Turn up a corner and check that all lines are transferred before taking off the carbon.

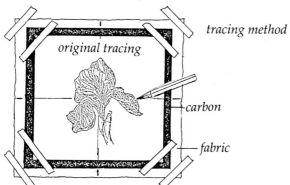

tracing method

original tracing

carbon

fabric

See-through method for transparent fabrics

Lay the fabric over the design, secure it with tape, and trace round the lines with a sharp B pencil. If the fabric is very soft, use a fine brush and watercolour paint, keeping the brush as dry as possible.

If the fabric is translucent, the design can be taped to a window or placed on a sheet of glass over a source of light.

Sewing method

Trace the design on to tissue paper. Position it on the fabric, right side up, and secure with pins or tacking, (basting) threads. Sew along all the lines through the tissue with small running stitches. Score the tissue along the lines to split the paper, then pull gently away.

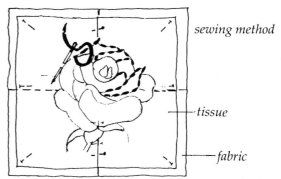

sewing method

tissue

fabric

Template method

Trace the design on to stiff paper or thin card. Cut out the shapes and lay them on the fabric. Mark round the outline with running stitches, or washable embroidery pencil. In quilting, the shapes are laid on the fabric and scratched round with a needle, (see page 27).

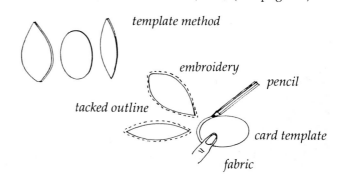

template method

embroidery

tacked outline

pencil

card template

fabric

Poppy prints by Jacky Hodgkiss.
The basis of the design is prints made by dipping the top of a poppy seed capsule in paint and printing it on to calico. Embroidered in chain stitch, French knots, buttonhole, and straight stitches.
6 in (15 cm) square.

Montbretia by Marion Brookes.
Designed from sketches, transfer-painted on to paper and then ironed on to cream polycotton. Embroidered in surface stitchery and some quilting.
4 × 7 in (10 × 18 cm).

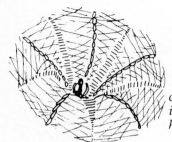

convolvulus flower worked in stem, straight and herringbone stitch

daisies in straight stitch with knot centres

Surface stitches

Flowers have been subjects of embroidery for so long that certain stitches have become associated with them, like long and short stitch for petals, and French and bullion knots for centres and tiny buds.

Traditional techniques were the result of long experiments to find the best use of fabric and thread for that particular purpose, but today most embroidery is done for effect rather than for use, and the choice of methods and materials is much wider.

Fabric

As a general rule, fine work needs fine smooth fabric and heavy work needs a good supporting fabric.

Threads

These should pass through the fabric easily, but difficult textures can easily be couched or whipped round other threads.

Needles

Have a variety of crewel needles, so that you can choose the right size of eye for the thread.

Frames

Straight stitches and couching are best on a frame, other stitches like stem, chain and eyelets are easiest to work in the hand.

chain stitch

stem stitch

14

Ideas for stitches

Some well-known stitches are shown here, with a few suggestions for their use. You can learn the basic technique from a stitch dictionary, or one of the small paperbacks which are published by manufacturers of embroidery threads, but the ways in which these stitches can be used are legion.

A certain amount of practice and experiment is therefore necessary. Every stitch can be adapted to many different effects. You can alter the direction, the scale, and the type of thread. You can work a stitch in circles, in lines or in blocks; you can spread it out, use it singly or pile it up in a heap. Many people master a few basic stitches and use them all the time.

It is rewarding to study the work of the past, and embroideries of all kinds can be found in museums, exhibitions, in the the auction room, (at a preview you can often handle the items), or in illustrated books. Exhibitions of contemporary embroidery are an excellent source of new ideas for stitches.

herringbone stitch

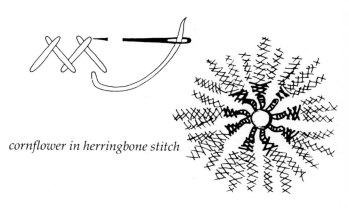

cornflower in herringbone stitch

bullion knots

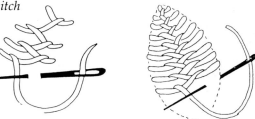

fly stitch

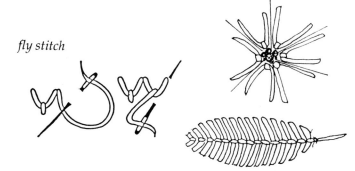

cretan stitch

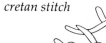

buttonhole stitch

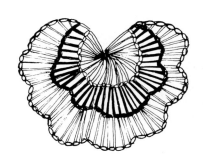

french knots

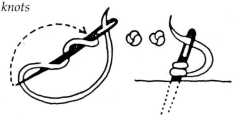

15

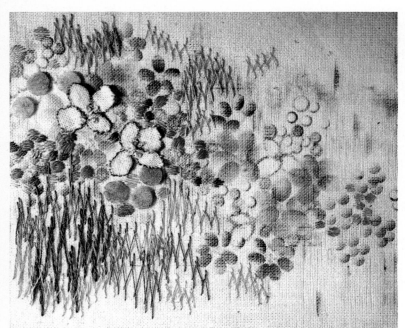

Meadow flowers by Marion Brookes.
Design taken from a sketch and transferred freehand to calico with a poker pen. Singed petals, added punched circles of painted non-woven fabric, embroidered in cretan and satin stitch.
4 × 3 in (8 × 10 cm).

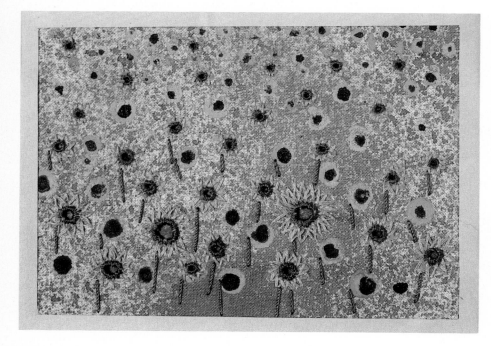

Field of sunflowers by Linda Cook.
Design adapted from a photograph, and transferred freehand to the fabric with pencil. The calico background was first sprayed with paint, and then embroidered with eyelets and straight stitches.
5½ × 4 in (14 × 10 cm).

Yellow flowers by Sandra Elms.
Design derived from pattern exercises. The transfer-painted design was ironed on to canvas and organdie, and some flower shapes were embroidered on to each layer – mainly straight stitches, satin stitch and French knots.
7 × 11 in (18 × 29 cm).

Shading stitches

The kind of meticulous shading stitches which produce a realistic effect have not been in fashion in recent years, but if you are happier with a needle than with a brush then it is most rewarding to embroider a favourite flower in this subtle technique.

Design

Designs should be as realistic as possible. Make a tracing of your drawing or photograph, marking the direction of the grain and veining of the flowers and leaves, and pencilling in the shadowed areas.

tracing made from a photograph of an iris

Fabric

A firm, matt, closely-woven fabric makes the best background. Choose a colour and tone to complement the design.

Threads

Loosely twisted silk, stranded cotton or crewel wool are all suitable. Wool is the easiest to use. Silk gives the most lively effect as it reflects more light. Stranded cotton and wool can be highlighted with silk. Threads can be mixed in the needle. Choose a variety of subtle shades approximating to the natural colours of the flower, with the addition of very light and very dark shades for highlights and shadows.

Frame

Though it is possible to work small pieces in the hand, beginners should always use a frame, preferably a fixed frame where both hands are free, (see page 30).

iris design transferred to fabric by tracing method, with some lines worked in split stitch

Transferring the design

Use dressmakers' carbon, (see page 11) to transfer the tracing to the fabric. As the whole area will be covered by stitchery, you can mark direction lines in carbon or pencil on the fabric, and indicate colour and shadows with crayon.

Where a petal or leaf turns back, the change of stitch direction may not be obvious from the working drawing. A solution is to cut out the shape in tracing paper, mark the lines radiating from the growth point, and fold over the edge.

turnovers

Long and short shading stitch

The effect of successive rows of this satin stitch is a smooth surface which flows round the natural curves of the form, reflecting light from subtly blended colours and tones.

Long and short derives its name from the first row, which consists of alternate long and short stitches. Colour is blended by the needle coming up in successive rows through or between the stitches of the previous row.

Start and finish with two tiny back stitches. Fill in one petal at a time, working from the back towards the front, building the flower up in layers. A thin line of split stitch will give a more sharply defined edge, and help to build up an impression of depth.

First row: this outlines the shape. Make alternate long and short stitches up to the edge, bringing the needle up in the centre of a shape, and down on the outline (or over the split stitch outline). Work outwards from the highest point of each shape and fan out on either side, angling the stitches towards the growing point. Where the curve is acute, tiny wedge stitches can be fitted in to keep the correct angle.

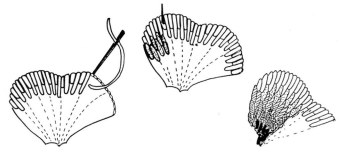

Second row: Use a deeper or lighter shade as required. You can either come through each previous stitch, splitting the thread, or come up between the previous stitches if the thread and needle are very fine, and then take the needle down again in the direction of flow. Keep the stitches approximately the same length, and the lower edge of the row irregular. Subsequent rows are worked in the same way, using a different shade of colour.

The last row: This will be in the darkest/lightest shade. You will have to miss a few stitches if the row is being fitted into a diminishing area.

split stitch

Turnover

These are indicated by outline, and by a changed stitch direction. The fold can be accentuated by oversewing to raise it up, or by a deep narrow shadow just beneath.

turnover worked in padded satin stitch

Highlights and shadows

Even with a very exact reproduction of colour, the finished embroidery can sometimes appear rather flat. This is where the question of perspective comes in. Does the work give a clear impression of form and distance? Look carefully at your original source of design, noting that rounded areas catch the light and turnovers and receding areas create shadows. On closer observation, you may find that a highlight that you had thought was a lighter shade of the prevailing colour is, in fact, a tiny area of brilliant white, and conversely a shadow may not be a deeper shade but a totally different colour. Accentuation of these features may make your design spring to life. The very best way to make sure the design is lively is to work from a freshly picked flower.

Needle-painting

This is simply a freer version of long and short stitch, worked in a much greater variety of threads, mixing silk and wool, cotton and metal thread.

The technique is exactly the same and the outline is worked in long and short stitches, but the filling can be done with any length of stitch.

The effect is still that of graduated colour and light and shade, but the texture is more varied. Some areas can be worked over a second time to raise the contours.

When building up several layers of stitches, stronger shades can be inserted at key points with very fine thread and needle that will not make obvious holes, the stitches being stroked in very carefully between the rows.

Pansies by Marjorie Lawrence.
Design taken from an illustration in a garden catalogue, transferred to linen twill by the tracing method with dressmakers' carbon. Worked in long and short stitch in a single strand of embroidery cotton.
6 in (15 cm) square.

RIGHT
Poppies, daisies and clover by Nettie Spink.
Design traced from own drawing, transferred by tracing method with dressmakers' carbon. Worked in crewel wools in long and short stitch.
9 in (18 cm) square.

Shadow work

In shadow work the design is embroidered on the wrong side of sheer fabric, producing a shadowy effect on the right side. The technique is extremely simple, but the result is sophisticated. White on white designs have a fragile and frosty look, whereas coloured designs change accordingly to the fabric and thread; worked in cotton on organdie they appear matt and smoky, but worked in silk thread on crystal organza they achieve a pearly opalescence.

Shadow quilting is another technique which makes a similar effect with sheer fabrics, (see page 26), and the two methods can be used together.

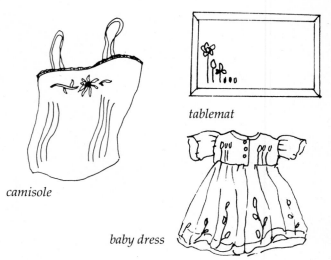

camisole

tablemat

baby dress

abstract iris design in shadow work by Val Tulloch.

Ideas for use

Small shadow work designs need not involve a great deal of sewing and making up, as they can easily be embroidered on bought items such as lingerie, table mats, blouses or delicate baby wear.

Design

Shapes should be kept simple with smooth edges and no interior detail. As they have to be worked in herringbone stitch, they should also be fairly narrow. This is particularly important for an article which is going to be worn or used, as long threads may snag in the wash or catch on the iron.

Large areas can be broken up in several ways – they can be subdivided, outlined with double lines, or filled in with smaller decorative shapes.

Extra lines, details, and small motifs can be added with surface stitchery on the right side.

Where washability is not essential, the design can be enhanced with shadow shapes in fabric as well as stitchery, with painted areas, and with shadow quilting.

ways of breaking up large areas

Fabrics

Sheer natural fabrics such as organdie, lawn, muslin, chiffon, silk, crepe de chine, organza and georgette are used, as well as suitable synthetics. White or very pale pastels show up the coloured thread best.

Threads

Threads need to be in bright colours to show through the fabric. Use a matching fibre such as cotton on cotton and silk on silk. A single strand is the easiest to manage and keeps the light quality of the technique.

Transferring designs

The design should be clearly but lightly traced on the back of the fabric. Use the see-through method or the tracing method, (see page 11). Alternatively, there are many small floral sprays available in transfer sheets which are suitable for shadow work which can be ironed on to the back of the fabric. Choose the light coloured inks.

Technique

Small pieces can be worked in the hand, larger pieces in a ring frame, (see page 30).

Use a sharp crewel needle, begin and end with a tiny double running stitch, and try to start each section with enough thread to finish it.

Although the embroidery can be done from either side, working from the back is generally considered easier. Closed herringbone stitch is used, which appears on the front as double running stitch.

Working from the back, fill in the shapes with closed herringbone stitch, taking alternate stitches at the top and bottom of the line. The size of the stitch is adapted to the fluctuating shape. Where the design develops curves on one side, the outer stitches will be slightly larger than the inner ones.

Working from the front, fill in the shapes by working a running stitch alternately each side.

When the 'shadow' part of the work is complete, the design can be further embellished by surface stitches on the front. Stem and back stitches are used for lines, and padded satin stitch for filling in small areas.

closed herringbone stitch

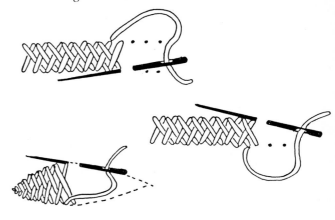

double running stitch

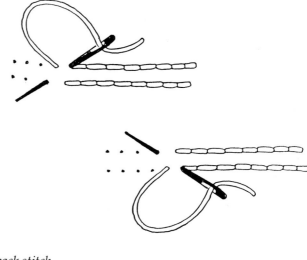

back stitch

23

Shadow work panel by Alana Coombes.
Design based on Art Nouveau illustration, transferred by direct tracing. Worked on organdie in fine silk twist.
5 × 8½ in (12 × 22 cm).

RIGHT
Clematis by Pauline Bannon.
Shadow work, designed from drawings and transferred by the sewing method. Worked on organdie on the wrong side in stranded cottons using two threads, with added French knots and straight stitches on the right side.
5½ × 7in (14 × 18 cm).

Quilting

Quilting is a method of stitching two or three layers of fabric together and enclosing a filling, which produces a raised surface pattern. The work is usually done in one colour, as changes of tone can be produced by the density of the stitch patterns.

Shadow quilting is worked in the same way, but using transparent fabrics and coloured fillings.

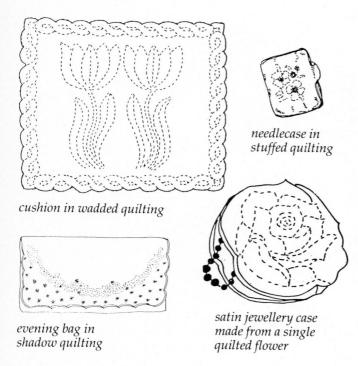

cushion in wadded quilting

needlecase in stuffed quilting

evening bag in shadow quilting

satin jewellery case made from a single quilted flower

Uses

Wadded quilting provides warmth, and is used for bedcovers or warm clothing; it also provides padding, which is useful for cushions, heatproof mats, and soft containers like jewellery rolls. Shadow quilting is purely decorative, but very pretty for cushions, evening bags, lingerie and table linen.

Wadded quilting

This is the traditional English quilting, and consists of a filling between two layers of fabric, all three layers being stitched together in an all-over design.

A shadow version of this is to sandwich pieces of coloured felt or bright fabric between two layers of transparent fabric, and outline these with running stitch.

Design

Designs for quilting often consist of simple repeating units. After the outlines have been worked the shapes puff up gently, so that a linear design on paper becomes a series of embossed forms. Think in terms of raised areas rather than of outlines.

All-over flower designs can be built up from templates. Motifs are often linked with a formal grid pattern or scrolling lines.

Fabric

Fabrics containing a large percentage of natural fibres are recommended, as wholly man-made fibres are often too springy. A plain pale fabric with a sheen will show up the pattern best.

Filling

Synthetic wadding is available in various weights, and is light and washable. A thin layer of woollen fabric or loosely knitted interlining can be used. Felt, foam and cotton wool are not recommended as they tend to go lumpy or disintegrate with use.

Threads

Match to the colour and fibre of the top fabric. A strong quilting cotton can be used on cotton or linen.

Needles

Use the short needles called 'betweens' in an average size.

Frame

Quilting should always be done on a frame if possible, (see page 30), as the layers need to be kept smooth and flat and well tacked together. You can secure the backing fabric to a home-made frame, spread over the wadding and then smooth over the top fabric. Pin lightly, and then tack all three layers together all over, starting from the centre. Keep the tension slack, so that the rounded shapes can take up as much fabric as necessary while they are being worked.

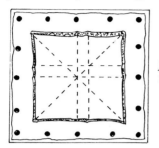

fabric tacked ready for quilting

Transferring the design

The design can be drawn on the top fabric with a washable embroidery pencil or sharpened dressmakers' chalk before being framed up, or it can be transferred to the top layer by the template method, (see page 11), after being framed up. Template shapes can be laid in position and marked round with chalk or the point of a needle – the indentation should show up long enough for the line to be worked.

marking round a template with a needle

Method

The design is outlined with running stitch which looks the same both sides. Back stitch can be used if the item is not reversible. Work from the centre of the piece outwards.

Take the needle through all three layers with every stitch. Either stab back and forth with a hand each side

of the frame, or, when you become accustomed to the work, take up three or four stitches at once on the needle.

Stuffed quilting

This method is also known as trapunto quilting. This uses two layers of fabric. The design is outlined in stitchery and the shape is then stuffed with wadding or coloured wool from the back, so that the shapes stand out in relief in the top fabric.

Fabric

The backing fabric should be firm and closely woven, because if it is too soft, the relief design will appear on the back of the work instead of the front. The top fabric should have a slight sheen and a gentle pliability.

Filling

Odd pieces of synthetic wadding can be used, or scraps of yarn, or natural wool such as is used for chiropody

Method

The design is transferred to the back of the work by the see-through or the tracing method, (see page 11). Sew round the outlines through both layers with close running stitch. Large simple designs can be worked on the sewing machine.

Working from the back, make a small slit in the centre of each outline, and stuff the shapes to the height required. Close the slit with overcasting or herringbone stitch.

stuffing shapes from the back

Quilting and printing by Celia Litchfield-Dunn.
Flower design traced on to backing, worked in back stitch from the front, and stuffed from the back. Transfer-printed leaves with split stitch centres.
6 × 4 in (15 × 10 cm).

LEFT
Quilted flowers by Celia Litchfield-Dunn.
Design derived from pattern exercises, traced off and transferred by the tracing method. Wadded quilting, worked on ivory satin in silk thread, with added eyelets and beads.
6 in (15 cm) square

29

Frames

Ring frame or embroidery hoop

Ring frames can be used in the hand, or they can be clamped to a table, fixed on a stand, or have a wooden leaf which can be tucked under the thigh – thus leaving both hands free. A ring frame consists of one wooden ring fitted inside another, between which the fabric is tensioned, the stretched fabric surface uppermost.

Lay the fabric, right side up, over the inner ring. Press the outer ring over it. Pull the fabric out gently until it is taut, being careful to keep the grain straight, and then tighten the screw. Bind the inner ring with cotton tape for fragile fabrics.

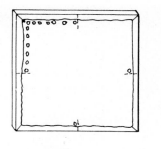
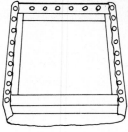

fabric on the front of home-made frame

fabric folded to back of home-made frame

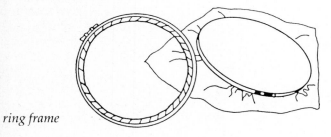

ring frame

Home-made frame

Many embroiderers use home-made frames, and panels are often left on the frame afterwards, thereby saving stretching and mounting.

They are made of four pieces of wood joined together. The fabric is attached to the frame with staples or drawing pins, (thumbtacks), on the front if the frame is temporary, or at the back if the work is to be left on.

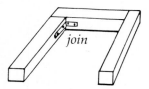

join

Finishing off

When the embroidery is finished it will have to be stretched, and then mounted or made up. Think about signing and dating your work: pieces of embroidery are kept for decades, and it adds greatly to their interest and value if future generations can identify the embroiderer.

A panel, well framed behind glass, should last at least 100 years, provided it is made of suitable materials and is protected from damp, dust and too much light. Many textiles in the past have deteriorated simply because of the materials used for mounting and framing.

For mounting, use hardboard rather than cardboard which may contain harmful acids and absorb damp. Always look for 'acid free' materials.

Lace the fabric on to the mount rather than glueing it. If you prefer adhesives, use one made of polyvinyl acetate and make sure none of it touches the design. Cover the back of the mount with cotton fabric, and seal over the stitching with strips of self-adhesive masking tape.

Seal the glass into the frame, and when the mount is in place seal all round the edges at the back of the frame, before covering the whole back with brown paper and sealing this with brown gummed paper.

Stretching and pressing

This is the process of damping the fabric and setting it in shape, before it is mounted or made up. It is not applicable to all kinds of work, but it squares up the fabric and 'irons' it without flattening the stitchery. Work taken off a frame may not need stretching. Quilting is never stretched. Shadow quilting can be given a gentle press from the back through a cloth. Small pieces of embroidered fabric can be pressed face down over a folded cloth. Larger pieces should be properly stretched as follows:

1. Place some sheets of wet blotting paper, or wrung-out flannel or towelling, on your drawing board.
2. Pin lengths of string across the board, outlining the required finished size.
3. Place the embroidery within these lines, right side up. Using rustless drawing pins (thumbtacks) pin and stretch the fabric to shape, starting at the centre of each side and working outwards. Check measurements and ensure that the sides are at right angles.
4. Leave it to dry naturally, for however long it takes.

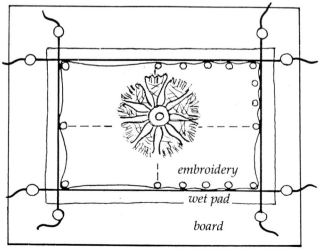

embroidery

wet pad

board

stretching

Mounting

If it is to be a panel, the embroidery should be mounted before it is framed.

Cut a piece of hardboard the required size. Mark the central vertical and horizontal lines. Lay it on the back of the embroidery, fold over the fabric to the back matching the centre lines, and pin from the centre of each side to the corners. Add more pins and keep checking that the front looks all right. When the corner is reached, trim the fabric and fold it down.

The fabric can now be glued or laced over the hardboard. Lacing is easier to adjust. Using a long thread, start in the middle of each side and work outwards, first vertically and then horizontally. Keep adjusting and tightening until the fabric sits square on the face of the hardboard and fits snugly all round. Cut a piece of cotton to cover the back, turn under a small hem and stitch down.

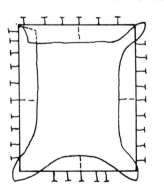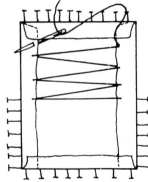

mounting

Acknowledgements

First published in Great Britain 1988
Search Press Ltd
Wellwood, North Farm Road,
Tunbridge Wells, Kent TN2 3DR

Photographs by Search Press Studios

ISBN 0 85532 618 2

Typeset by Scribe Design, Gillingham, Kent
Made and Printed in Italy by Amadeus S.P.A. Rome

Trail of flowerheads by Linda Cook.
*Designed from pattern exercises, photocopied and ironed on
to cotton fabric. Petals outlined with metallic pen, filled with
paint and scraps of fabric, centred with embroidery. The
larger petals are worked in stuffed quilting. (Also shown on
page 1)*
14 × 4 in (35 × 10 cm).